The Story of Sue

by Curtis Washington

Glenview, Illinois • Boston, Massachusetts • Chandler, Arizona
Upper Saddle River, New Jersey

Sue on exhibit at the Field Museum of Natural History in Chicago

It is almost never foggy in South Dakota, but it was foggy on that August day in 1990 when Sue was discovered. Susan Hendrickson would be the one to find her—the largest, most complete, and best-preserved *Tyrannosaurus rex* skeleton that has ever been found.

T. rex (short for *Tyrannosaurus rex*) is the world's most popular dinosaur, the largest and fiercest meat-eater ever to stomp the earth. Sue was to become the most famous *T. rex*. This is the story of how she was found and of what paleontologists are learning about her.

---

paleontologists: scientists who study fossils to learn about prehistoric life

Peter Larson in the field

The fossil-hunting season was almost over. Only the most dedicated bone hunters from the Black Hills Institute remained. They were keeping their eyes open for any rock formation in the area that might hold more fossils of dinosaur bones. They especially hoped to find a T. rex. No one on the team had ever seen T. rex bones in places where people search for fossils.

Peter Larson, the head of the Black Hills Institute team, had loved bone hunting since he was a young boy. One day, when he was four years old, he bent down to pick up a fossilized tooth in a ditch near his house. He didn't know what it was, but he knew it was very interesting. From this early age, Peter's dream was to have a dinosaur museum in his home town in South Dakota. He and his brothers made that dream come true. When they grew up, they founded the Black Hills Institute.

Susan Hendrickson at the museum with Sue

The foggy day when Sue was found in 1990 did not start out well. As Peter sat and ate his breakfast, he noticed that one tire on his truck was becoming flat. He would have to go into town to have the tire fixed. The rest of the team decided to take a break from the hard work and ride with him. It had been a long season, and people were getting tired of the dry wind, dust, and heat of South Dakota. Susan Hendrickson did not go with them. For two weeks, a rock formation near their camp had been calling to her. She couldn't stop looking at it. She had a strong feeling that something special was buried on that 60-foot, golden cliff. That day offered her a chance to check it out.

True Adventurer

Susan Hendrickson is a real-life version of an adventure movie hero. When she dresses for work, some days she puts on scuba gear. On other days, she wears jeans and hiking boots.

She began her career diving for tropical fish in Florida. After that, her next jobs were raising sunken boats, hunting for amber on tropical islands, and hunting for meteorites in the mountains of Peru. "I'm just a person who loves finding things and learning everything about them," she has said. Finally, in the late 1980s, Susan met Peter Larson, who asked her to help hunt for dinosaurs. That's how she ended up in the camp on the day the truck tire went flat.

Susan knew the golden cliff was only about a two-hour walk away, but there was a problem: it was too foggy to see the cliff from the camp. She would have to find her way by memory. She set out with her trusty dog, Skywalker. "I told myself, 'Don't walk in a circle,' but that's just what I did." Two hours later, she was back at the camp! At that point, many people would have given up and waited for the rest of the team to return from town. But Susan was determined. She waited for the fog to burn off and then headed out again.

This is what a dinosaur fossil looks like before it is dug out.

Susan and Skywalker kept their eyes on the golden cliff in the distance and reached it about midday. She started her search by walking along the bottom of the cliff. She wanted to see if any bones had come out of the cliff. At about the midpoint, she found something. She saw bones at her feet and looked up to see where they had come from. Just above eye level she saw them: large bones that could only have come from a large dinosaur. Could it be a *T. rex*?

Susan hurried back to camp and showed Peter Larson two bone fragments that he immediately recognized as coming from a *T. rex*. "I could not speak. I could not believe my eyes," Peter said. Peter and Susan were so excited they ran all the way back to the golden cliff. Not only was it a *T. rex*, but it looked to Peter as if it could be the most complete *T. rex* fossil that had ever been found. "I'm naming it after you," Peter said. "I'm calling it Sue."

A scientist carefully cleans Sue's jaw bone.

Getting Sue Ready to View

The Black Hills Institute team worked overtime to remove Sue from the rock. They finished the job in about three weeks. Now the really hard work would begin. For an almost complete dinosaur, thousands of hours would be needed to clean the bones, repair the fragile or damaged ones, and decide exactly how they all would fit together if the animal were still alive. The team spent many months carefully working on the dinosaur skeleton called Sue. All the while, Peter Larson thought about how he would finally be able to fulfill his boyhood dream. He was going to open a dinosaur museum in his home town, and make Sue the main attraction.

But by May of 1992 his dream began to fall apart. Sue was becoming well known, and a dispute about who actually owned the fossil began. Peter had paid $5,000 to the owner of the ranch where Sue was found. But other people also claimed to own the land. Eventually, the courts decided that the *T. rex* bones would be sold at auction. In 1997 the Field Museum of Natural History in Chicago, Illinois, bought Sue for more than $8 million. The museum finished the job of preparing Sue for exhibit, and the world finally saw her in 2000. Visitors to the museum have been amazed and thrilled by the ferocious *T. rex* ever since.

Tyrant Lizard King

At the time Sue was found, she was only the twelfth *T. rex* fossil ever discovered. She was also the largest and the most complete, with about 90 percent of her bones remaining. Because of this wonderful discovery, paleontologists have been able to learn much more about *Tyrannosaurus rex*, the fearsome dinosaur whose name means "Tyrant Lizard King." This "king" lived 67 million years ago in swampy regions full of other creatures to eat.

---

auction: a public sale

Sue's teeth

People are fascinated with *T. rex* from what they've seen in movies, but you wouldn't want to meet one in person! A *T. rex* like Sue weighed about 14,000 pounds. Sue's skull alone was 5 feet long and weighed 600 pounds. She was 42 feet from head to tail. Her 58 teeth looked like 12-inch-long bananas, only much sharper. The *T. rex* was so ferocious and powerful that its enemies were probably other *T. rexes*, not other dinosaurs.

Questions About Sue

Until Sue was discovered, paleontologists had not found an important *T. rex* fossil in almost 100 years. A new, well-preserved, and nearly complete *T. rex* caused great excitement. Here are some of the questions paleontologists are trying to answer as they study Sue.

Is *T. rex* Related to the Eagle?

The group of birds called raptors, or birds of prey, includes eagles, falcons, owls, and hawks. They are skilled hunters. All of them are meat-eaters and have excellent vision. Unlike most birds, raptors grab their food with their claws, not their beaks.

This is what some paleontologists think a *T. rex* parent and baby looked like.

Some paleontologists think birds of prey are descendants of a group of meat-eating dinosaurs known as theropods. *T. rex* was a theropod. They point out similarities in the bones of both groups of animals, as well as the similar traits of eating meat and being excellent hunters. They also point to evidence that a feathered theropod has been found.

But other paleontologists think the theropods are related to all birds, not just birds of prey. They say that all bird skeletons resemble those of the theropods. For example, they all have hollow bones. Some believe that a *T. rex* baby was covered with feathers and was taken care of by a mother or father, the way young birds are cared for by parents. Theropods also had a special bone similar to the wishbone we see in modern birds. Sue's wishbone, however, was thicker than your arm.

As birds of prey such as eagles and hawks fly, they hunt for food. From great heights, they can see small animals far away on the ground. People sometimes describe anyone with excellent vision as **"eagle-eyed"** or **"hawk-eyed."** Scientists wonder whether dinosaurs that hunted, such as *T. rex*, had keen vision. Do you think some day people will call anyone with good distance vision "dinosaur-eyed"?

Was Sue Really a Female?

No one knows for sure, but some paleontologists believe Sue really was a female. Males and females of the same species often are different sizes. For example, male gorillas weigh twice as much as female gorillas. In some species, females are larger than males. Female birds of prey are larger than males. If *T. rex* really is related to birds of prey, then *T. rex* females also could be larger than males. And Sue, the largest *T. rex* ever found, therefore most likely would be a female.

How Old Was Sue When She Died?

Some paleontologists have noticed that *T. rex* bones have growth rings, like the growth rings that tell the age of trees. By looking at Sue's growth rings, they found that Sue was about 30 years old when she died.

You and Sue

With all of the tools and techniques available now, paleontologists expect to learn a great deal by studying Sue. If you had the chance to study Sue's skeleton, what would you try to find out?

Extend Language   Dinosaur Name Origins

When scientists find a new dinosaur, they give it a name that describes what the dinosaur was like. They use words from the ancient Greek and Latin languages. (Latin was the language used in ancient Rome about 2,000 years ago.)

Here are some dinosaur names and what they mean.

Tyrannosaurus rex "Tyrant lizard king"
Greek: *tyranno* = tyrant
Greek: *saurus* = lizard
Latin: *rex* = king

Theropod "Beast-footed"
Greek: *thero* = beast of prey
Latin: *pod* = foot

Use a dictionary to find out what these dinosaur names mean.

stegosaurus	ankylosaurus
ornithopods	sauropods